THE BEASTS

poems by

Meg Files

Finishing Line Press
Georgetown, Kentucky

THE BEASTS

Copyright © 2023 by Meg Files
ISBN 979-8-88838-303-2 First Edition
All rights reserved under International and Pan-American Copyright Conventions. No part of this book may be reproduced in any manner whatsoever without written permission from the publisher, except in the case of brief quotations embodied in critical articles and reviews.

ACKNOWLEDGMENTS

"The Beasts" poem first appeared in *Global Poemic*, May 2021

The quoted sentence on page 16 is from *The Outermost House: A Year of Life on the Great Beach of Cape Cod* by Henry Beston.

Maggie Nelson, excerpt from *The Argonauts*. Copyright © 2015 by Maggie Nelson. Reprinted with the permission of The Permissions Company, LLC on behalf of Graywolf Press, Minneapolis, Minnesota, graywolfpress.org.

Publisher: Leah Huete de Maines
Editor: Christen Kincaid
Cover Art: Karyn Kloumann
Author Photo: Picture People Studio
Cover Design: Elizabeth Maines McCleavy

Order online: www.finishinglinepress.com
also available on amazon.com

Author inquiries and mail orders:
Finishing Line Press
PO Box 1626
Georgetown, Kentucky 40324
USA

Table of Contents

The Beasts 1

The Veterinarian 2

One Cat One Dog 3

Black Swan 4

The Friend 5

I'm Dead Now What 6

Boogie 7

Back When We Were Beautiful 8

The Veterinarian 9

The Friend 10

Coyote 11

Done For 12

At First 13

Porthole 14

The Veterinarian 15

The Chorus of the Beasts 16

Childhood 17

Fires 18

Flail 19

The Friend 20

Oh Sweet 21

Bobcat 22

The Friend 23

The Veterinarian 24

The Peeled Planet 26

*For Gina,
daughter of my heart*

THE BEASTS

The creatures, clothed and unclothed, are in the ruins—
yes and the tango skeletons naked beneath gossamer—
here they are in the world with us sequestered. They
will inhabit our stadiums, the band shells, a cabana—
it's not that before they were afraid but uncurious—
and now caped antelope, the furred wild turkey, a
gowned coyote wander our streets. We forget we are
animals here inside. You sharks, you spotted deer,
mountain goats, wild boar, puma—you are costumed
but we do not see you. So what, you say? What's new?
They enter the school without uniforms except for
the knee socks, they levitate onto desks, bite books.
Unknown, unknowing, we hide in the CVS though
the beer and the tampons are endangered. The ghosts,
the ghosts in their lingerie boogie to silent beats. Do
they know each other, the creatures and the ghosts?
We, inside, cannot know. But our mates are nodding
on couches, and some wine still resides, and we have
abandoned our costumes. The creatures have satisfied
their lack of curiosity and are returning to the forest.
The ghosts in their chassé hang with the creatures. We
fools in sweatpants have forgotten that we are animals.
Go ahead, when this is over, the beasts are telling us,
try to live in your ruins. The monsoon has come at last.
Adiós, we would say, but we understand your word. So.

THE VETERINARIAN

He died on election day. He knows what he said, to aggravate the family, but even now he's not sure how he would have voted when he stepped up to the booth. He's heard his daughter say, *I was with my dad in hospice on election day, and I always liked to vote in person, somehow it feels so good and right though no more, but anyway, I didn't vote and I'm here to say it's not my fault.* They changed him into clean different colored tee-shirts. They checked the catheter. The morphine. The harpist played Amazing Grace and some other harp-stuff, and he didn't mind.

And look at all the animals now. He'd known animals, of course, he'd been a veterinarian, large animals, cows and horses, and even camels once and elephants and sacred cows. But look at these desert creatures out in the streets.

And his daughter, moved from the big house to the guesthouse behind it, in her grief. *Well, my girl, who among us didn't know grief... your mother and those others after, but of course your mother.* The empty streets, the animals at the mall.

He doesn't miss much now but his wife always knew what he needed. And now, he has to say, he almost misses a good B.M.

ONE CAT ONE DOG

In all their loneliness and loss and grief, they'd needed comfort animals, and the shelters were riven of their dogs and cats, the cute young ones but also the old needy ones. Some pot-bellied pigs. It was mutual need. Nobody knew what happened to the puppy-mill puppies, maybe cast out into the desert, maybe added to the shelters and adopted as mutts by the lorn humans.

And after their people were gone, the leftover humans took them in, until every live dwelling kept precious and spoiled moppets and darlings—your terriers, your collies, your spaniels, your setters, the designer goldendoodles, bishonpoos, and that famous breed, the Arizona Brown Dog. Cats were inside, safe from coyotes, with their carpet trees and garden catnip.

Her father, the large-animal vet, had allowed her one cat and one dog. She used to cry out that when she grew up… at one point she had four cats, three large dogs, and a goat. Then she grew back down to one cat, one dog, until now with the yard and guesthouse menagerie.

The caged birds fell.

And the remaining humans were snug and sad in the fastness of their domesticity.

BLACK SWAN

The perigean full moon was imminent, with its high tides (who cared, in the desert), with its closeness to earth in its elliptical orbit, with its golden beauty rising as if from the mountains. This one didn't have a name, that anyone now knew, nor the internet cared to guess. Before Times? Super Worm Moon, Super Pink Moon, Super Flower Moon, Super Strawberry Moon. So she named it herself, the Super Derelict Moon—as if the moon, etc., had abandoned them, not the other way around.

In the Super Derelict moonlight, she rode her bike to the open-air mall. She didn't know why. It was in riding distance, it was civilization. It was sad. She knew it was empty in the daytime, six-foot markings chalked onto the walkways, a few security guards. Now it was haunted by javelinas. A herd of maybe twelve, a squadron, their young reds along, these bristly compact bodies with their little eyes and no necks and pink-button snouts. They don't grunt or woof at her—is she maybe one of them? They can't see her clearly, and perhaps they can smell her scent glands. No prickly pear at this mall. Also none of the trash people used to lure them with—oh, weren't they exotic, and weren't their reds adorable, and weren't you amazed at the bites taken out of your prickly pear, and didn't you oddly adore their stink? Come on in, here's Victoria's Secret where you can try on a Satin and Lace Comi Set or a Lace-up Romper, and here's Soft Surroundings for your Blissbus Balboo Shorts.

THE FRIEND

K. also died before. Now she sees them all, her leftover big poodles, her dear dear dear friends, her spiritual guide (the painting in the living room, his eyes following everyone). K. knew her friend hadn't yet known the depth of their friendship upon the diagnosis. Before—at school, *may I show you the way.* In the kitchen—*have this cheese toast. I put extra avocado in the salad for you.* Later—*Find a music student for my piano.* So now she goes to her friend as she can, mostly in dreams. She says: Look at this new yet-to-be-published author, here's the title and name, and let this be proof. On waking, her friend remembers the dream but can't catch the title or author, fret as she does and does. K. sent her friend who needed to be helpful but didn't know how to the store for winged maxi-pads—not so much that they were required (anyone could have picked them up) but so her friend might understand what was imminent. Not that it worked. At the end, her friend did know it was the end, she was in a coma, she supposed, but she listened to her friend read her own poems to her—her dogs, her leavetakings. Now, K. wants to dream her friend the love, not too late, after all, and she wants to say: look around, these empty streets, the mall of javelinas, the beasts in costume I have still to dream to you. The books I will dream to you. She knew it was imminent. We both are still here.

I'M DEAD NOW WHAT

She started to post on Facebook when he got sick but stopped when she got too many followers. She was nobody but almost famous. Pray for him, they said, although she didn't believe in prayer (or gym workouts or yoga or gardening or…). She thought about dressing up as a hospital worker to see him. It was three and a half months. They each had an "I'm Dead, Now What?" book that they'd separately filled out. She hasn't looked at his yet. She kept a journal, and here it is:

• D.'s fever spiked. I hate that word "spiked." There's way too much spiking going on. Before, he never got sick. Before the spiking, he'd tried to conceal the aches. Then the coughing.

• This morning D. said, What's that smell? What smell? I say. Can you smell rain coming? No, he says, it's the smell of nothing, nothing at all. I've heard of that, and so I try him on a spoon of salsa. Nada, he says, sick but himself nevertheless.

• Today he wants to know what's going on with the animals. We no longer have any animals, I remind him, not to worry him. As if he didn't know about the backyard graves. But he wants to know about the wolves and if anyone is still shooting them. The coyotes and the deer and the fires and the elephants. And I quote.

• This morning D.'s lips were blue. I got him into a tee-shirt and sweats and brushed his wild hair and drove him off. What could I do? They wouldn't let me stay with him. They said they'd call but so far nada.

• So now the CT scan shows respiratory inflammation. The voice says it's "ground glass opacity." What the hell? It's like your shower door, I am informed. Fluid and debris. This is what it has come to: my beloved's lungs are our shower door.

• Today there are grim milestones and another grim record. Grim, grim, grim. Things are razor thin. I wish there were actually an abundance of caution. What, indeed, is going on with the animals. I have taken to sleeping on his side of the bed. I smell him on his pillowcase.

BOOGIE

Deer are in the streets at night, though there's no foliage there. They have already munched up all the grass in the yards of the idiots who have lawns in the desert. They like, for the moment, taking to the streets, alone. The houses are dark, and the human creatures have forsworn the seasonal wild lights of their rut, or whatever it was. Some are reddish-brown but also some are blue-gray—the seasons are befuddled. The antlers grow velvet but then the bucks rub it off. The spotted fawns are in triplets now. They have the mesquite leaves and beans, and the desert is theirs now. They flash their white rumps to the hunters with their new hobby licenses. Huh huh. Here is your asphalt, have it. For the duration (whatever that is), the deer and the coyotes and bobcats and mountain lions put on their costumes and boogie together.

BACK WHEN WE WERE BEAUTIFUL

The old photos in the albums she has taken to the guesthouse confirm: his semi-long dark hair, his dear handsome profile, her long blonde hair. Their hippie headband, crop top, hip huggers. Little did they know. Did they know they were beautiful? She doesn't think so, now. Camping on the Flattops, with the young husky and the diabetic cat who needed daily insulin… an orange tent, a campfire, a propane stove, no other humans, and she ran off, while he read against a log with a beer, in some sort of ecstasy, flinging her arms and singing the theme of Tchaikovsky's Violin Concerto at the top of her lungs, with no one to hear, ecstasy. Who says you can't sing it? Was the world still young then too? Before the knowledge of the deep change? She knows every couple had its stray and its indelible memories—and that they changed as time shifted. Well, so? They were mated. And so? The terrestrial topknotted quail will scurry in their pairs, with the adorable (as attributed by humans) trail of chicks.

She thinks the human creatures will probably stop pairing up, once the remaining pairs are broken up.

THE VETERINARIAN

He knew about natural selection and its love of virus strains that do not kill hosts. Come here, come here, embrace your friend, who walks around and embraces her other friend who coughs in the grocery store. Millions die along the way but so it goes along the path to mutation and survival. But he was no longer available to talk about viral zoonosis, not that the people would have thought that applied to them. He was a large animal man, whose creatures didn't exactly embrace each other. Ask me about rabies, he wants to say, foot-and-mouth, myxomatosis (intentionally released in Australia to knock out the rabbit infestation—though they became immune, so there!), the parvovirus which came from cats and jumped to the poor dogs with no resistance and African hyenas and then to lions—cats to dogs to cats. He sees his daughter trying to do the research, and he can't help her. He wishes she'd move back into the big house. She can't live there until the man comes home, probably. And he himself understands shutting down in a small place at the end. Finally, he'd pretty much confined himself to his single bed. As for politics, he'd loved to stir the pot. And now?

THE FRIEND

K. who was forever scrupulous when it came to graywater and recycling. And joining a buffelgrass team. And now? She sees them in their drought. She sees them, who used to take their cloth bags, filling up the trunk with plastic grocery bags. She who took her own Tupperware to the restaurant for leftovers sees the takeout Styrofoam. Her friend, hidden now in her own guesthouse, had never found K. righteous, despite her own lax habits. She wants to tell her friend: driving emissions are falling, though diesel is stable. Electricity is down in the buildings but not at home. Air quality is up but not carbon dioxide emissions. The scientists are stuck at home, so who knows? The skies are clear. Even now, she wants to write another letter to the editor.

She could soar around and beam in the news of jackals in Tel Aviv, puma in Santiago, pink flamingoes in southern France, dolphins near the Bosphorus shorelines, lions sleeping on the road, monkeys in the palace in India, raccoons in Central Park, mountain goats in Wales, leatherback turtles in Florida. Yes, and oh joy newborn North Atlantic right whales.

Of course, the holed-up humans just wanted to believe all that. Truth is, the swans in Venice were there all the time, and those dolphins in the canals? Those photos were from far away out in the Mediterranean Sea. The humans put themselves in detention. They'd already estranged themselves from the creatures, and wasn't it pretty to think the creatures would come out to play?

Just look, K. might suggest to her friend. Let me show you how to look. Maybe show you it's not too late. Here's another photo from your (alive) dear friend: *A Dawn Again*, a desert sunrise.

But loving her, she won't beam to her friend in dreams: it's too late, it's over, we blew it, we did ourselves in. Look: *A Dawn Again*.

COYOTE

D. is sedated. A nurse has held up an iPad so she can see his head, with the tube in his mouth. He looks like himself asleep and snoring, when she'd wake up ahead. But not really. Is he in there? Poor outcome, she reads.

She becomes a coyote. It lies on the desert side of the back fence behind the guest house, snugged into the soft dirt beneath the palo verde. Is it sick? injured? ready to give birth?

She drops to all fours. She is reddish gray and she has buff underparts. But that's not right, for she wouldn't be thinking of her own long legs and black tail tip and nose pad and prominent ears.

She is the super canid runner, up to 40 mph. She can leap 14 feet.

She is hungry. Packrats and rabbits. But no cats.

The coyote lies by the back fence behind the guest house for three days. When it runs, it carries its tail down.

Then she is human again. Her love has a tube inserted into his trachea. Poor outlook. What can she say to the iPad?

When her father was dying, in his coma, she kept saying I love you, I love you, what a wonderful dad, please know that always, always.

At dusk, the coyotes begin their yips and barks and long howls.

DONE FOR

D. is not how he thinks of himself, just her shorthand, which he has seen in her journals that, yeah, he snooped in. He never learned anything he didn't already know. She still didn't like Hank Snow but had come around to Faron. He was the love of her life. She didn't like his garlic breath. She loved their lovemaking, she missed their sex. Their house was basically his, and she didn't mind, he lived there too, she'd say. There are wolf and buffalo representations. There are their pet graves. He supposed he was done for. Their story had its details, just as everyone's did. Their first apartment, the run-over puppy, their own music that nobody else could duplicate ever, the years of photo albums before they stopped printing the phone photos, oh what did any of that matter, he was done for and he couldn't say to her that every touch and detail does matter, the dolphins, the orange tent in the mountains, the snap-button shirt he wore on their first date, the years of Christmas trees and the irreplaceable ornaments (but who would care). Why did you love me? he wants to ask around the tube in his mouth. What I loved about you: just you, my personal human love on this earth. *Hello, love.*

But he's done for. After his life in words, is that the best he can do, done for?

His last day at their home: Trying to read for distraction, can't remember what now. Light, not enough light—and scrolled up the blind behind the chair. Oh god, what is that? Desert mouse hanging from the chain link fence behind the window. Snout with pink nose and whiskers, back of head desiccated dark matter. Stretched neck, furred body about to drop, a tier of tiny ribs on the side. Tail and legs drooping. Decomposing from the head down.

He hopes she will not open that shade for a year. Or, suffused with fever, maybe he just conjured that scrap of death.

AT FIRST

At first, the empty streets were haunted but almost romantic. You could set it to music (and they did), the barren shelves, the half-built structures, the abandoned volleyball net in the park, the Attention Customers signs. We'll Get Through This Together at the closed art theater. No traffic on Speedway, at all. Did they miss their tourists? Maybe not. Forget a soft reopening. The city was for the moment theirs alone. The palo verdes were in radiant bloom.

At first they were inspired by the balcony musicians in Italy, with their opera singers, guitars, accordions, dancing, pan lid cymbals. The balcony tiers of musicians just broke her heart. In the desert, one neighbor and then the next, et cetera, stepped outside at 10 p.m. and rang a bell. It's just a neighborhood, and it doesn't last, but it's sweet for the moment. Someone brings out his saxophone.

As a fox, she roams the city. The thing about being a fox is that she knows she is gorgeous in hue and brain. Others may not know about their white throats, but she does. Oh but she adores herself. She brings her kits out of the drainpipe at the abandoned arts center, where she'd thought to keep them safe. They now forage by day. She always knew she could forage in trees, but now she does so. Still, she leads the kits through the city, that they should know. Look here, my little ones, look here and here. Know and remember. Never a drainpipe, even if we used to emerge to enchant the early-morning humans preparing the gallery before the crowds. Now we shall return to the brush.

PORTHOLE

The big house was theirs, more his, maybe, with the buffalo skull and the wolf pictures, but she'd fixed up the guest house. Spare but sweet. She opened up the futon to sleep on and folded it back up to sit on in the day. What had been the plan? Well, for visiting company. So a small TV, a table, two chairs, a bookcase with a little library of duplicates and cast-offs. She painted one wall blue and sewed curtains. A little dollhouse! A casita! She'd finished it just before any guests could travel and stay. Was it portentous? It was just a project, wasn't it? Making a playhouse in the back yard? She could not have known that he would leave the house, that she could not be there without him.

Waiting, in her dream, they are in a hotel room, and she gets up while he lolls. She goes to him again and again, leans and caresses his face, arm, back, as she gets dressed, does her hair, in preparation for leaving—on a plane, she thinks. The room is airy, suffused with white.

Subtle, she thinks, upon awakening, sub-tle.

Waiting, she reads paragraphs over and over, her attention elsewhere, or nowhere. She picks up the books, she pulls them from the shelves in their big house, because how to fill the time? But nobody would say she's reading them. She can't catch anything on the little guesthouse TV, and in the big house, she has no clue about all the remotes on the coffee table. He'd been the master there. Oh and so many lovely elsewheres. Even if her friends would wrinkle their brows at *master*.

The desert is silent. She hits the side of her head, to knock out *deathlike silence*.

Although the little porthole clock she'd taken from her father's condo tocks from the guesthouse's small table. She cups it in both hands and looks into it. Through it is a tropical cloud build-up at a sea's horizon. And now a nearing island. No. She submerges into deep gray-green water.

THE VETERINARIAN

His last lady friend lived across the cul-de-sac and would come over in the evening with her glass of wine while he had his nightly gin and tonic. Her husband was long gone. She had—has!—a wrought iron cocker spaniel in her courtyard, in memory of her Buster. She told him that in the middle of the long moonlit nights, sleepless, she'd go into the courtyard with a glass of wine. He never asked her what she thought of but now imagined that if he had done that it would be his young wife. But he himself never went out into the moonlit yard in the middle of the night. Though sometimes he roamed the condo. After he died, he heard her making sure to his daughter that they hadn't been sweethearts. The long-gone husband and Buster lived with her still. There are photos of them with his arm around her and them holding hands, but he supposes there are sweethearts and there are sweethearts. His daughter found the unopened blue pills container when she cleaned out his place. He thinks she was sort of in admiration. The non-sweetheart moved to another state to stay for the rest of the duration with her daughter's family. She has a spot of her own, he can see, and he loves it when, at her age, or whenever, she drives the tractor. She has the wrought iron dog with her still. Oh, and look, when she was a teen she flew an airplane from a farm field in Illinois.

There aren't that many to watch. The son-in-law for a little while, though the end is in sight.

He spots his young wife's clock, that was in their bathroom for so long, on his daughter's little table, a round Bulova like a little porthole. The hands spin, as if to indicate the passing of time in an old movie, without having to fill in all the intervening events, before skidding to slow present time for the rest of the story. He remembers the small tocks as his wife put on her face. Now his daughter sets that little clock beside the guesthouse door, outside.

THE CHORUS OF THE BEASTS

Animals Don't Love Humans (YouTube):
Cheetah, African Buffalo, Bison, Fox, Cougar, Rhino, Lion, Jaguar, Tiger
What the hell?
YouTube?
We're attacking your Jeeps and your fences and your cage bars.
Look upon our stripes, our muscles, our spots, our grasses, our horns.
Right, animals don't love humans.
All of us don't love you. Okay, your dogs and your cats. Maybe. Not your ferrets. Your aquarium fish and desert tortoises? We have to eat what you feed us.
One of your own told you about us: *They are not brethren, they are not underlings; they are other nations.* There is more but you get the idea.
But did you listen? Nooooooooooooooo.
And those videos you see of us helping each other out? Bear saving drowning crow. Lion saving baby wildebeest. Baboons with antelope, orantugan with chicken, and oh the baby elephant and baby giraffe. People, people. Even we can tell it's fake. What is the matter with you? But then it seems there's no end to the folly and fakery you will believe. Why? We don't know. Because for some perverted reason you want to, we guess.
We do know each other. Nothing sentimental about it. We are not here, now, to teach you any damned thing, about the natural world, about the ecosystem, about the laws of nature. You fools. You fools. You fools. This has nothing to do with you. Except with how you have fucked with us. But it's over now, or soon.

CHILDHOOD

The night Buster was killed... Everyone let their pets roam in those days, and Buster was known for making his neighborhood rounds. How exactly did it come down? It was night. Did she find him out in busy Portage Road, already hit? She doesn't think she actually saw the hit. Her dad carried him to the basement. He must have had a heart attack, was what he told her—not, we shouldn't have let him out next to a busy street. Maybe heart attack was correct. She sat by him on the rec room floor, and wept and wept. The first death.

At camp, she and her bunkmates sneaked out to the hidden forbidden brambles and filled their bucket hats with blackberries. At lunch and dinner, they sneaked extra bread, smeared it with butter, poured sugar over it, folded it, hid it in their bucket hats, and later in their cabin devoured that sugar bread. Always hungry. She found a tiny mouse abandoned in a nest under the cabin and tucked it into a matchbox with a little cotton from a pill bottle, tried to touch a fingertip of milk to its mouth. That pink naked creature didn't take long to die.

Her mother's been gone too long to see what's happening. She who couldn't quite explain to her schoolkids that incest didn't apply to gerbils. She who pep-talked her daughter into doubt, she who assigned her approval to D., she who died saying either I can't breathe or See you soon, depending on the story. The soft body.

How insignificant what stays with you: a dead cocker spaniel beside a ping pong table, a dead pinky in a matchbox, sugar bread, a mother's gentle burps followed by "excuse the pig," her lipstick kissed onto a square of toilet paper.

FIRES

Last year it was the *non*soon, but this year, in the drought, the storms decided to rain down. No small rain here. Last night, she woke to the giant lightning/thunder/torrent. The dog needed to go out but was afraid. The cat was under the bed. She went under the big house's patio to take it in, and oh how to take in the swept beauty, though fearful animals, though entubated beloved. Maybe all will endure?

She goes to the library, curbside pickup. She leashes up the dog and hits the riverside trail, behind the library. Nobody is anywhere. How can she even be checking out books? When she can't talk to him. All their years and years of books. The river is running for the moment. She remembers their riverside trail walks, and when she said she liked the smell, and he said, well, that's the wastewater treatment. It is a spicy/sad smell now. Still.

How can it be, newsfeeds, emails, stupid motorists swept away in flooded washes, wildfires wildfires, grocery stores restocked, supply chains disrupted, orders and deliveries, interviews, revelations, mostly everything carrying on, when D. was not.

But deer are photographed standing in the ashes. (Everything is not carrying on.) Mudfloods from the burn scars. (How long will the internet, etc., last?)

It will wind down. It will be over.

FLAIL

She reads about the end. *They flail. Their eyes fill with terror.*

Dear heart, dear heart, I see you. I don't suppose you see me. Goddamn iPads, goddamn them to hell and back and bless them, she supposes. You are here yet. I know what you're telling me. But we are both here. Still and yet.

A scrawny bear cub wanders the roads alone. Presumed an orphan, sow burned up.

Wolf hunters overshot the harvest quota. Much enthusiasm among wolf hunters this season. She wants to expunge the words *harvest quota* from his ears, if ever they were there. Please, you do not need to be thinking of wolves in your extremis.

Today on the way to the mailbox—there is still mail!—she sees a lizard so much the same color as the sand as to invisible, except that she did see it, and a dead snake, head mostly gone/devoured, except for a glittering eye, a Sonoran shovelnose, she thinks. She wants to tell him. It's not that she wants him to know about the lizard, the snake—she wants to be able to tell him. That is all. She wants to tell him everything.

THE FRIEND

The obituary said "She went to her glory." That was a joke that no one got but the one who wrote it. Yes, we used to make fun of euphemisms and platitudes in obituaries. "Joined the angels," "gained her wings," "entered into her reward." So my obit writer thought it would be clever to make fun. As if I could be in on the joke. When he asked my friend what she thought about the wording, after the fact, of course, she had her doubts. This was my friend? The obit writer tried to explain the joke to her. She doesn't know: was he a true friend with the joke? Would he be (for the duration)? *Oh my friend, my beloved friend who didn't know. I am sorry. I didn't have a say. Or maybe you're laughing in your glory. And your large poodles landed in a good place. It took some doing. But I like to think you know. You have no idea how I miss you. But, truly, I think you do. You foresaw the missing.*

She asked me once if I'd wanted to be reincarnated as a dog. We did love them so, and sometimes they did seem to be those we'd known. I tried to explain that wasn't how it worked, but she wasn't hearing me. And now here she is, alive yet, becoming foxes and coyotes. Oh my true friend, I think we both understand that at this point you miss me much more deeply than I miss you. I wish I could help. I wish I could tell you about glory. I wish I could say the end is not in sight. I do still care, in my way.

OH SWEET

He does see the desiccated desert rat. But that is not the last image. He is going to be disappeared from the face of the earth. What an expression. The face of the earth. But not from below the earth. Or not from the air of the earth. She probably won't take him to the water of the earth. Whatever she plans to do with him. They hadn't made plans. He supposes he won't be disappeared from there. She'll take him to the mountains, he's pretty sure.

What? A zillion moths flooding him from the purple flower bush outside the door, wolves his wolves, the suede fringed "buckskin" shirt his mother made him, the sound of something like unknown heavy machinery in the near distance, the smell of her hair, Huck on his raft, no life flashing before his eyes, the pencil against the writer's hump on his finger, Come back Shane, girls in straight wool skirts up at the pencil sharpener, no secrets because after all he is just himself, the dawns he rose and left her in her sleep and the glory of the sunrise and the tenderness of leaving her in bed, the small cry of a cat *I hear you, sweet,* his body his bestirred penis, the way her old father in his last months kept saying I'm just so tired and his attachment to his bed, could anyone get all the dead Roys singing together at his memorial, no secrets because after all he is just himself. He is underwater and can't swim up and get his nose above water, the summer night that could never end until here it is, he turns, he vanishes from the face of the earth.

BOBCAT

In the parking lot, she's out in the car crying. He won't be disappeared from her. From the face of her.

When she is a bobcat, her face is a little too small for her body, and so is her tail. Not that she herself thinks so, or can even see herself. Still, that tawny body, black spots, ah. You, humans, can know me by my tracks—lobed at the rear and concave at the center, scalloping.

Yeah, you named me for Stubby. I hide up in my clefts and go for little critters. I cry out in screams. I will be grayer, come winter. Who doesn't love my tufted ears, n'est-ce pas?

Ah, she can't keep this up. She is weeping in the parking lot. She is the compact body of the bobcat, but of course she is the beloved, bereft of her beloved.

THE FRIEND

What she wants to tell her friend, weeping in the hospital parking lot:

- Big poodles are the most wonderful beasts… I know, I know, they're dogs and you have lost your beloved.

- You will take in many many beasts of the canine and feline sort, and who knows, maybe some others, because you will need the beasts and they will need you.

- I heard you reading my poems to me at my deathbed. Do know.

- I had many many friends. You didn't always or maybe often remember whom I was talking about, there were so many, though you faked it. You were among them, deeply among them. Probably they heard your name more than you heard theirs. Probably they faked knowing you. It doesn't matter. You were all on the face of the earth.

- I hate to tell you, but the end is in sight. I tried to do my part (graywater, buffelgrass), but it was nothing really. My spirit was there. I did roadside cleanup. Things are winding down. When I got my diagnosis, I was oddly relieved. Something was seriously wrong, I knew, no matter what I'd been told. And then I knew. My end was in sight. No need now to sort the piles of mail. No need to settle anything. A grief, a relief. And you, now, still here, this is the same: the diagnosis is terminal, and what you all should do is not to give it up. Yes, keep up your mitigation efforts, for sure. That is required. You don't have to say or know that we're done for. But.

THE VETERINARIAN

What he wants to tell his daughter, weeping in the hospital parking lot:

• It was always the big animals for me, but now I have come to see the quail (with their trail of chicks), the cottontails, the gila monster with its beads, oh all the lizards, try to keep the dogs from the toads, the tarantulas and wolf spiders (do not be afraid), the Black Witch Moths (maybe be afraid, if you read the legends, not that I was ever a one for legends), the ringtail and the coati (that I know you saw once each), yes the bobcat, yes the fox, yes the coyote, yes the collared peccary, of course your red-tailed hawk pairs, the Gila woodpecker on your chimney.

• Your mother, your mother, your mother. She took that picture of me in the kiddie wading pool with little you pouring water on my head, you in your saggy underpants. Your mother. See you later, she said. It remains to be seen. And I don't suppose I will have any way to tell you.

• On the farm: We kids always worked. We boys had pissing contests out the window. Our father was sometimes rough, in a farmer's way. Our mother got her hair caught in a chickenhouse fan and was scalped and in the hospital away from us boys for months and came home and wore a bad wig for the rest of her long life and cooked us tongue and shoofly pie. We all grew up, if that's what it's called, to animals.

• I had no sentimentality about animals. I know I know. I made your husband mad that I was prepared to key your dog if he growled at me. I didn't, did I? Animals were my life, and so somehow I must have loved them, even their mastitis, the feel of their flanks and udders and eggs.

• At the end, I was just so tired. That's what I kept saying, to your exasperation, I'm just so tired. Maybe that's the way it will all go. Just so tired.

- The human animals, anyway. Maybe I am qualified to note, from my history and present stance: The rest of the animals, sleeping their way through our dominion as best they could, will shake themselves awake. I was a Lutheran, and I still know the words: *Let the earth bring forth living creatures according to their kinds: cattle and creeping things and beasts of the earth according to their kinds.* Of course, I understand now, and maybe always, that those are human words. I have no right to ask, but, daughter, when it's the end, send the humans to bed, and loose the animals to do their moving through the waters, their flying, their creeping, their burrowing, their swarming. Let them have the waters and the heavens and the firmament. Me, never a sentimentalist (except later I cried whenever your mother was mentioned). Me, farm boy, cast back. Oh, go to sleep, hush now.

THE PEELED PLANET

Back in the guesthouse, she tries to read while she weeps, and this is what she finds:

"While we talked we said words like *nonviolence, assimilation, threats to survival, preserving the radical*. But when I think about it now I hear only the background buzz of our trying to explain something to each other, to ourselves, about our lived experiences thus far on this peeled, endangered planet. As is so often the case, the intensity of our need to be understood distorted our positions, backed us further into the cage."
—*The Argonauts*, Maggie Nelson

She can't think about any of this, but the sentences soak into her skin.

She lets the dog out. She lets the dog in. She is afraid to sleep in her cage. The pyres in India. The refrigerator trucks in New York. The disturbing, anomalous protrusions of blooms up and down the saguaros. Taking her picture, he'd direct: Knockers up. Those goddamn fashion masks she'd bought: dolphins, her favorite, until not. The Lone Ranger mask she'd got him, that he never needed. She would never touch anyone ever again. Anyway, no person.

She opens the clip a friend sends of wolf pups learning to howl. She is weeping. She watches those little blunt faces turning up their heads trying to copy the pack, the mewling howls and little shrieks. Oh come look at this, love, my wolf man.

Outside at night: the wind chimes that her friend had given her and that she had managed to hang up with a ski pole, a chorus of coyotes, a siren.

A columnist she liked wrote about a man who wasted his life, wasted the "incandescent miracle." She copied that and printed it out in blue to adorn her desk. And she looked at it every every day. She didn't always remember, though.

An end: She tries to be one of the beasts, among them, but she cannot. She tries to see her friend. She tries to see her father. She almost thinks she can. Her back yard is full of pandemic dogs.

Her house is full of pandemic cats. She has moved back into the big house for them. D. is everywhere. Her own end is in sight. What is left? Miracles? Glory? How to look. How to see. No one understands these things. And this is the way it ends.

Meg Files is the author of the novels *Meridian 144* and *The Third Law of Motion, Home Is the Hunter and Other Stories, The Love Hunter and Other Poems,* the poetry chapbook *Lit Blue Sky Falling,* the novella *A Hollow, Muscular Organ,* and *Writing What You Know,* a book about using personal experience and taking risks with writing. She edited *Lasting: Poems on Aging.* Her awards include a Bread Loaf Fellowship. She taught creative writing, directed the Pima Writers' Workshop, and chaired the English and Journalism Department at Pima College for many years. She was the James Thurber Writer-in-Residence at The Ohio State University and the Doris Leadbetter Writer-in-Residence at Victoria University in Australia. She directs the Tucson Festival of Books Literary Awards and Masters Workshop.

www.ingramcontent.com/pod-product-compliance
Lightning Source LLC
Chambersburg PA
CBHW022126090426
42743CB00008B/1030